INFORMATION WAVES

Shirley Duke

Rourke
Educational Media

rourkeeducationalmedia.com

Before Reading:

Building Academic Vocabulary and Background Knowledge

Before reading a book, it is important to tap into what your child or students already know about the topic. This will help them develop their vocabulary, increase their reading comprehension, and make connections across the curriculum.

1. *Look at the cover of the book. What will this book be about?*
2. *What do you already know about the topic?*
3. *Let's study the Table of Contents. What will you learn about in the book's chapters?*
4. *What would you like to learn about this topic? Do you think you might learn about it from this book? Why or why not?*
5. *Use a reading journal to write about your knowledge of this topic. Record what you already know about the topic and what you hope to learn about the topic.*
6. *Read the book.*
7. *In your reading journal, record what you learned about the topic and your response to the book.*
8. *After reading the book complete the activities below.*

Content Area Vocabulary
Read the list. What do these words mean?

amplitude
compression
electromagnetic waves
frequency
integrated circuit
longitudinal
microprocessor
modulation
oscillate
pixels
rarefaction
spectrum
transistors
transverse
triangulate

After Reading:

Comprehension and Extension Activity

After reading the book, work on the following questions with your child or students in order to check their level of reading comprehension and content mastery.

1. *How did the discovery of waves change the ways people communicate? (Summarize)*
2. *Why do amateur radio operators have restrictions? (Infer)*
3. *Do waves carry energy? (Asking questions)*
4. *How would your life be different if waves did not exist? (Text to self connection)*
5. *How do scientists and inventors build on each other's ideas to create new technologies? (Asking questions)*

Extension Activity

Watch a wave! You'll need a partner, a Slinky and some tape. Put a piece of tape on one Slinky wire in the middle of the toy. Give one end of the Slinky to your partner while you hold the other and walk away from each other until the toy is stretched out, but not too far. Once you are both standing still, quickly push the end of the Slinky toward your partner and watch closely to see the wave. Repeat several times and observe. What is happening to the tape?

Table of Contents

Early Communication

What do you do when you want to talk to a friend across town? Text? Call? Both are simple to do, but think about how people communicated before technology harnessed the power of **electromagnetic waves**. Written communication has been used since ancient times. The Phoenicians, an ancient civilization, developed a simple alphabet. Another ancient civilization, the Sumerians, used picture writing

Sumerian cuneiform is the earliest known writing system, dating back to about 8000 BCE. It developed from the pictographs and other symbols used to represent trade goods livestock on clay tablets.

Oral messages were important for quick communications. Messengers often ran messages to the recipient. Horseback provided a means for faster delivery. Eventually, post offices developed. Still, people often needed to send messages even faster. Over the centuries, the search for speedy communication evolved.

Joseph Henry
1797 – 1878

As writing communications developed, using electromagnetic waves for fast communication also developed. Joseph Henry's development of the first electric telegraph in 1831 led to a way for sending fast messages. Other inventors improved on this.

The telegraph uses electricity to send coded messages through wires.

Early telegraph lines were primitive. Soon, the use of two lines, one for sending and a second for receiving, improved message sending. In 1835, Samuel Morse developed the Morse code, which used dots and dashes for the alphabet, further simplifying message delivery.

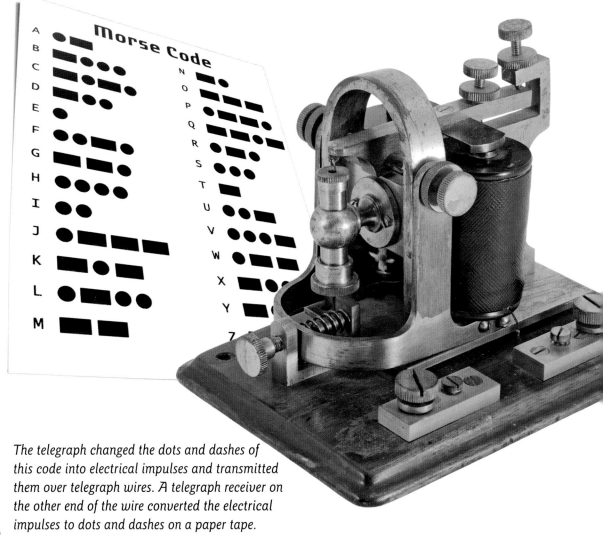

The telegraph changed the dots and dashes of this code into electrical impulses and transmitted them over telegraph wires. A telegraph receiver on the other end of the wire converted the electrical impulses to dots and dashes on a paper tape.

Great Britain adapted a form of Morse code used throughout Europe. As the need for international communication grew, the more complicated Morse used by the United States changed and adopted what was called the *Continental Morse*.

Guglielmo Marconi

1874 – 1937

The problem with telegraphs was that they were limited to the wires that transmitted them. There was no way to contact ships on the seas or reach other countries overseas, either.

In 1895, Guglielmo Marconi discovered groundwave radio signals. These radio waves moved around the Earth and could go long distances across land and oceans. This discovery first allowed waves to transmit information.

The Radio Act of 1912, a United States federal law, enforced limited amateur use of radio waves and required a license. It also assigned the frequency they had to use.

Guglielmo Marconi's ocean-crossing radio devices saved many lives, including all of the surviving passengers from the sinking Titanic in 1912.

Marconi sent radio signals across the Atlantic Ocean with high-power radios and giant antennas. He used information discovered by James Clerk Maxwell in 1873: the electromagnetic field, a **spectrum** of waves.

Many people began to use the limited radio wave space, called bands. Amateur radio operators, also called ham radio operators, communicated in relays at first, and by 1921, around the world. Wireless information was past its infancy and on its way.

Ham radio operators competed for radio air space, and those interfering with others' broadcasts were called "hams." Over time the term became common and no longer holds the original meaning. The correct term for operators is amateur radio operators. Amateurs must still be licensed and follow regulations.

What Are Waves?

Waves are a part of nature. People can comprehend the physical world better if they understand waves and their motion. People see and hear using vibrations and waves. Light and sound waves are the most familiar kinds of waves.

Sound Waves

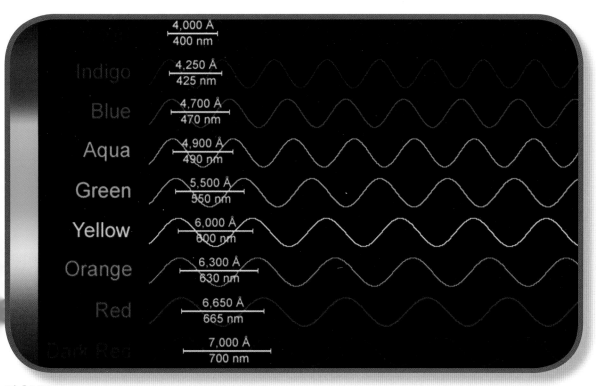

Light Waves

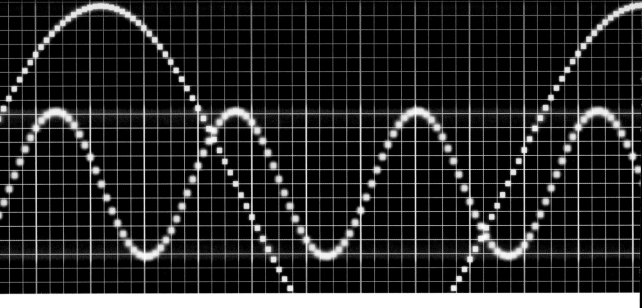

Waves have distinctive characteristics. They **oscillate,** or move back and forth, at regular intervals. A wave is caused by a force applied to matter. The force must continue to maintain the wave. A wave moves in a continually repeating pattern. Each wave has the same specific wavelength, **frequency**, and **amplitude** as long as the force continues.

Some waves are physical. Physical waves need a substance for transmission. Toss a rock in a pond. The force of the rock causes ripples in waves to move away from the center. Sound waves won't travel unless there is a substance to carry the waves, unlike electromagnetic waves.

compression   rarefaction

There are regions in the air where the air particles are compressed together and other regions where the air particles are spread apart. These regions are known as compressions and rarefactions. The compressions are regions of high air pressure while the rarefactions are regions of low air pressure.

Electromagnetic waves are a form of energy. Electromagnetic waves can move through a vacuum like space. These waves don't need a medium for transmission.

Wave motion is generated by particle motion. The energy of a wave is passed from particle to particle, while the particles do not change position.

Longitudinal waves move parallel to the direction the wave's travel. The primary waves of an earthquake are longitudinal waves. A **compression** is an area of molecules in a wave segment pushed closely together. A **rarefaction** is an area on a wave segment where the molecules are furthest apart.

Transverse waves displace the particles at a right angle to the wave direction. Water waves form with a combination of both.

transverse waves

longitudinal waves

Waves form in an alternating crest and trough pattern. This pattern is found in all waves. The crest is the high point of the wave and the trough is the low point. The distance between one crest and the next is the wavelength.

Amplitude describes the wave's height. It is measured from the midway point to the top of the crest. Amplitude shows how intense the wave is. Wavelength does not affect the amplitude.

Frequency shows how fast a wave is vibrating per second. Frequency is measured from the downward motion through an up cycle and then down until it reaches the same distance downward as where it began. The unit to measure frequency is the hertz (hz). Low frequencies have long wavelengths, while high frequencies have short wavelengths.

high frequency

low frequency

Though many waves can't be seen, they do carry energy from one place to another. A complex change in frequency will carry a signal from place to place. Waves are critical for transmitting information in a variety of ways.

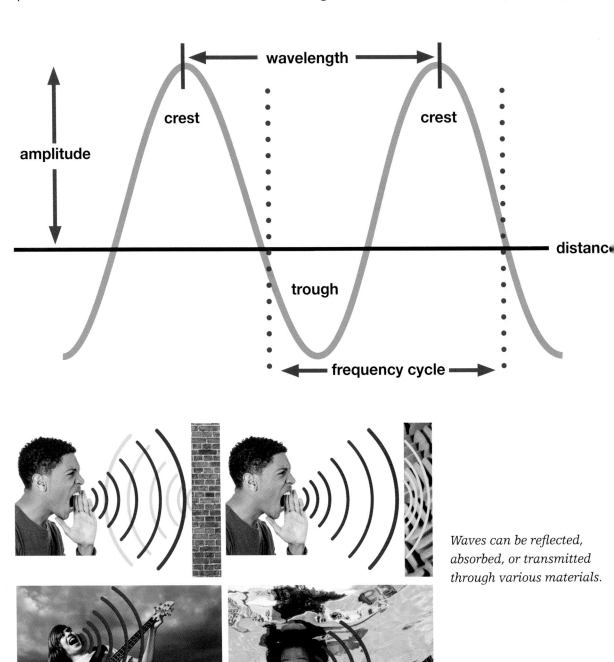

Waves can be reflected, absorbed, or transmitted through various materials.

Electromagnetic Radiation

Electrically charged particles in motion create electromagnetic waves, a ind of radiant energy. Another term is electromagnetic radiation.

These waves come from any source of energy. The sun creates huge mounts of radiation. The waves are formed by a magnetic and an electric eld. Electromagnetic waves travel through air and the vacuum of space.

Visible and Invisible Light

Most of the light waves in the electromagnetic spectrum are invisible to people. Only visible light can be seen. We see these as the colors of a rainbow.

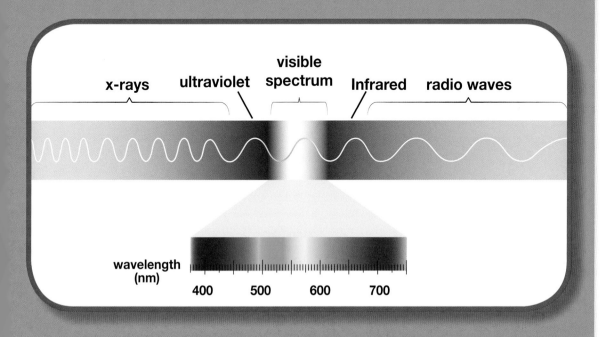

To make clearer signals, several radio telescopes are connected in an array. The Very Large Array (VLA) in New Mexico is made of 27 antennas set in a Y pattern almost 22 miles (36 kilometers) wide.

Charging particles by exciting them with electricity creates the glowing light seen in neon. Exciting means to elevate the energy level above a baseline state.

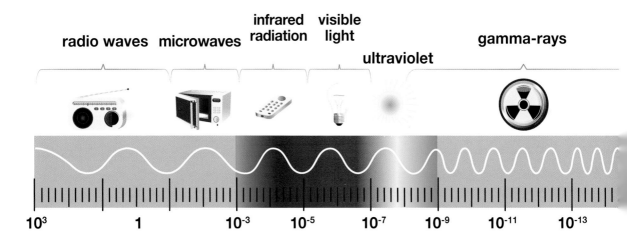

radio waves   microwaves   infrared radiation   visible light   ultraviolet   gamma-rays

10^3 1 10^{-3} 10^{-5} 10^{-7} 10^{-9} 10^{-11} 10^{-13}

Radio waves have the lowest frequency. Radio waves carry music, television, and cell phone signals. The signals are received by large radio telescopes, dishes made of metal that reflects the radio waves to a focal point.

Radar is an acronym for radio detection and ranging.

Doppler radar is used in weather forecasting.

Microwaves range from a few inches (centimeters) to a foot (30.48 entimeters). The longer microwaves are the kind found in microwave vens for heating food.

Microwaves can pierce haze, rain, snow, clouds, and smoke. This akes them useful for sending information to different places.

Radar sends out short bursts of microwaves. The echoes bounce back om the object to detect their location.

Skin Sense

Skin has nerve endings that detect differences in the amount of heat people feel.

Infrared light waves also vary in size. The longer, far infrared wavelengths are thermal, or have heat. A fire's heat and sunlight's warmth are infrared waves. Anything that has some temperature radiates infrared waves.

The shorter, near infrared waves aren't hot. These short wavelengths are used in television remotes to change your television channels. Infrared images also can be made with special cameras and film. The camera senses different temperatures and creates an image.

Fast Fact

Restaurants use infrared to keep food hot using special lamps that emit infrared waves.

Wave Watchers

Pit vipers have heat-sensing pit organs between the eye and the nostril on either side of their heads that can detect infrared light waves. It allows them to locate warm-blooded prey, even in the dark.

Visible light waves are radiation people's eyes can detect. The range of visible light extends from the long waves of red to the shorter waves of violet.

Prisms separate white light into each wavelength. The human eye detects the colors with receptors at the back of the eye.

The brightness of the color depends on the amount of light wave that is reflected, or what is sent back. Some materials absorb different wavelengths, making the colors people see.

White light comes from the combination of all colors.

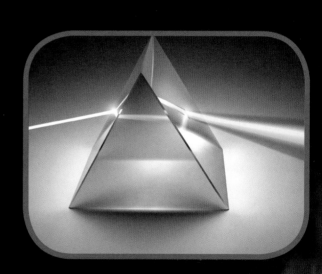

Did You Know?

People see colors because eyes pick up only the wavelengths that aren't absorbed by the object. For example, the sky looks blue because the sky absorbs all the other colors and only reflects blue.

Visible light, like other electromagnetic waves, travels through space. It is not made of matter, like sound waves or water waves, but of waves and photons. Light travels in a straight line, but it can be bent by different transparent materials, such as water, air, or glass.

Light hitting an object is either reflected, absorbed, or transmitted through that object. The material of the object and the light wave frequency determine what happens to the light.

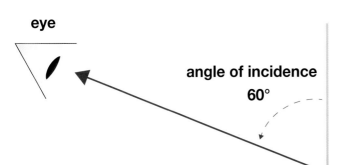

eye

angle of incidence
60°

air

apparent positi

water

40°
angle of
refraction

actual position

Ultraviolet light waves (UV) range in size, too. The shorter UV wavelengths contain more energy than the longer waves, which are closer in size to visible light.

The sun gives off UV rays of all lengths. These light waves are the cause of sunburns. Astronomers study UV light to learn more about the universe.

UV rays produced this image of the M81 Galaxy, 12 million light-years away from Earth.

Sun Block

The protective layer of ozone around the Earth's atmosphere blocks some UV rays. Scientists have created a UV index that lets people know how intense the UV light waves are.

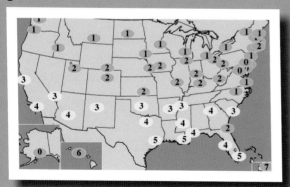

Exposure Levels				
Low	Moderate	High	Very High	Extreme
0 1 2	3 4 5	6 7	8 9 10	>11
Minutes to Skin Damage				
>60	45	30	15	<10

Heinrich Hertz
1857 – 1894

Heinrich Hertz, a German physicist, was the first to prove electromagnetic waves exist. His discovery added to James Clerk Maxwell's electromagnetic theory of light. The International System of Units (SI) unit hertz for frequency was named to honor him. His discovery made way for the wireless telegraph, radio, and television.

21

Accidental Discovery

X-rays were discovered accidently by German scientist Wilhelm Roentgen during other experiments. Roentgen took an x-ray image of his wife's hand and they were surprised to see her bones and wedding ring. Roentgen named this unknown radiation X.

Wilhelm Roentgen

1845 – 1923

X-rays have higher energy than UV waves because of their smaller wavelengths. X-ray waves behave more like particles than waves.

X-ray images are used to detect broken bones, but they can also show pneumonia and breast cancer. X-rays show images of the inside of the body in various shades of black and white. Different tissues absorb x-rays in different amounts. Bones appear white because their calcium absorbs the largest amount of x-rays.

It is important to limit exposure to the high level of energy in x-rays. Fortunately, Earth's atmosphere blocks x-rays.

The most energetic and smallest waves are found in gamma rays. Nuclear explosions and radioactive atoms give off gamma rays.

These rays can kill cells that are alive, making them deadly for healthy cells but useful for medicine, where they can treat certain cancer cells.

Gamma Rays

Some elements, like uranium and plutonium, emit gamma radiation naturally. The hottest parts of the universe give off gamma rays. Supernovas and atom destruction form gamma radiation.

Technology and Communication

Morse code and the telegraph led the way to new inventions. Marconi's early discoveries of radio signals paved the way for new inventions that used and improved upon those signals.

Alexander Graham Bell patented the electric telephone in 1876. After that, from 1877 to 1899, the technology for recording and playing back sound developed in a series of inventions.

Early phones worked much the same as today's phones: Your voice generates energy from the vibrations in your vocal chords. The energy travels into the microphone, making the diaphragm vibrate. The diaphragm converts the energy into electricity, which flows down the phone line to the speaker on the other end, where it is converted back to sound.

Fast Fact

In 1908, Columbia Records introduced the first double-sided records. Until then, all records were recorded on one side only.

The early 1900s brought the use of flat records in place of cylinders. In 1906, the RCA Victor Victrola record player was introduced. It could play records of differing speeds.

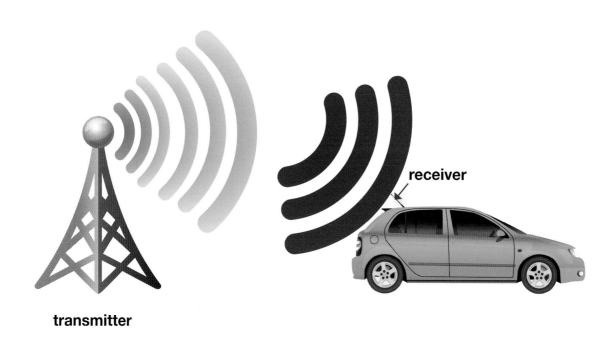

transmitter

receiver

Receivers

Antennas are metal rods or dishes that act as a receiver and capture radio waves. The waves are turned into electrical signals, which transmit to a radio, television, or telephone.

Antennas and transmitters are used for most modern communication systems.

The first radio broadcast took place in 1912. Radio signals are made of sound waves. Transmitters take electrical signals and change them to radio waves. These waves travel across large distances in a broadcast.

Wave signals are sent out through the atmosphere. They are picked up by receivers.

Radio waves led to the discovery of ways to control the frequency or amplitude **modulation**. This means varying the properties of waves. AM radio waves are amplitude modulation and FM waves are frequency modulation.

Evolution of Entertainment

From 1925 to 1949, radio was the most popular form of entertainment. Sound systems that put music and sound effects with movies came in 1925. The National Broadcasting Company (NBC) became the first radio network in 1926. The American Broadcasting Network started in 1945.

Radio stations are assigned a frequency that radio tuners can pick up. The tuning circuit selects that frequency and the current moves back and forth only at that frequency, tuning out other frequencies. The first radios with tuners for the different stations were introduced in 1916.

Frequency Units		
hertz	Hz	1 cycle per second
kilohertz	KHz	1,000 cycles per second
megahertz	MHz	a million cycles per second
gigahertz	GHz	a thousand million cycles per second

Space Communications

Spacecraft communicate with people on Earth using radio waves. The spacecraft has a transmitter and receiver and can interpret sent messages. Signals from both Earth and the spacecraft are weak due to the distance. Huge receivers focus on the exact location of the craft.

David Sarnoff, a leader in early radio, thought that pictures could be transmitted through the air. At the same time, Philo T. Farnsworth imagine a way that a picture could be broken into horizontal lines. The electrical signal of lines would reassemble into the same image on the receiver.

Farnsworth sent the first television picture in 1927. The tiny image was about one and a half inch (3.81 centimeter) square. In 1928, John Logie Baird transmitted a television signal across the Atlantic Ocean.

David Sarnoff
1891 – 1971

John Logie Baird
1888 – 1946

Farnsworth modeled his early television in 1928 to reporters. The blurry pictures arrived at 20 seconds per picture on a tiny screen. This motion was enough to make the viewers think their eyes were seeing motion.

World War II (1939–1945) halted television development. By 1947, a few regularly scheduled television shows were broadcast. The first **transistors** came about that year. Transistors are small electronic switches and amplifiers.

Fast Fact

Television was introduced to the public at the Chicago World's Fair in 1939.

Philo T. Farnsworth and Mabel Bernstein demonstrate a home television set at the Farnsworth Television Laboratories in Philadelphia, Pennsylvania 1935.

Philo T. Farnsworth
1906 – 1971

The first monitors used cathode ray tubes (CRT). Now, a liquid crystal display (LCD) and plasma form thinner screens for the picture reception. LCD is a technology with a display grid. A current is moved over two conductors on the grid. This controls the light for any point on the grid, called **pixels**.

How it Works

CRTs form images by sending electrons from the back to phosphors, a fluorescent material, at the front of the display. When the electrons hit, they light up and show on the screen. Red, blue, and green are combined to produce all the colors you see. The electrons are guided by magnetism.

Digital Signals

Digital means electronic technology that uses a positive or non-positive state, or off and on signal, represented by the numbers one and zero. Digital signals are more reliable than traditional broadcasts, which use electrical pulses. Most modern technology uses digital signals for transmissions and receivers.

Television cameras copy the picture it is viewing one line at a time. These multiple lines of colored light are changed into an electrical current, left to right and top to bottom. It moves to your television receiver and is reimaged as the picture sent. Microphones catch the sound and send it at the same time in a separate signal.

Television signals are transmitted at frequencies specific to the station broadcasting them. New technology uses digital signals. The numbers 0 and 1 in a digital transmission work like the information in a computer.

31

Network television began in the U.S. in 1949. The broadcasts were in black and white. Color televisions became available in 1954, but most people owned black and white television sets and continued to use them. Walt Disney's 1961 debut program, *The Wonderful World of Color*, spurred an interest in color televisions sets.

Evolution of Color TV

Color television technology was invented by 1950, but it wa primitive and couldn't be viewed with black and white television sets. Color television sets were sold beginning in 1954.

The decades between 1950 and 1974 brought changes in sound and broadcasting technology. This resulted from the Cold War years as the space race with the Soviets intensified. The **integrated circuit** (IC) grew from the need to fit electronics in space capsules. These ICs held thousands of transistors on one tiny chip.

Cable Comes Along

Time, Inc. offered cable television in 1972 as Home Box Office (HBO). The company bought rights to recent movies and sent them through satellite and microwave signals to local systems. The early cost of HBO was $6 a month. Cable television introduced MTV in 1981.

The introduction of satellites improved and refined radio signal transmissions. A satellite is a human-made piece of equipment that collects data or aids in communication.

Satellites receive radio signals sent from Earth. They return the radio signal to Earth, often by reflecting off the satellite. Modern satellites receive radio signals and return them to Earth stronger than the original signal. This is called amplification of the signal. These satellites can change the frequency to another one so the signals don't mix.

Communications satellites work as a relay station. Ground stations transmit signals that the satellite's receiver picks up. The signals are filtered and their frequency is changed and amplified. It then sends the signal back from a transmitter antenna. Satellites have improved wireless communication through technology.

Modern Communication

In 1914, the first cross-country telephone call took place. Phones could be installed in cars by the 1940s. By 1973, the first cell phone system was developed, but it would be another ten years before cell phones were sold.

The Brick

The first handheld cell phone on sale to the public, the Motorola DynaTAC 8000X, was purchased in the U.S. on March 13, 1984. It cost nearly $4,000! It was so big and heavy, its creators nicknamed it The Brick.

As technology improved, the smartphone, a cell phone that functions like a computer, significantly changed communication.

Cellular phones are used within a cellular network. Voices are changed to an electrical signal in the phone. This signal is sent out as radio waves. The receiving phone changes the signals into sound. These phones work as signal transmitters and receivers. However, the signal that can be sent from a portable phone has a short range.

The Anatomy of a Smartphone

Smartphones generally include a touchscreen, Internet capability, camera lens, video-streaming, and a system that can run applications (apps), along with the capability of communication by phone or text. Technology advances will continue to improve smartphones in the future.

The cellular network divides regions into cells. A cell is hexagonal sections with a base station, or phone mast. These huge receivers pick up the cell signal from a phone. The mast relays the signal to the next phone mast in the direction of the person being called. This rapid transmission allows calls over long distances.

Limited numbers of frequencies for radio waves makes another problem. The sending and receiving signals need separate frequencies. Cell networks reuse frequencies of other cells as they move from mast to mast.

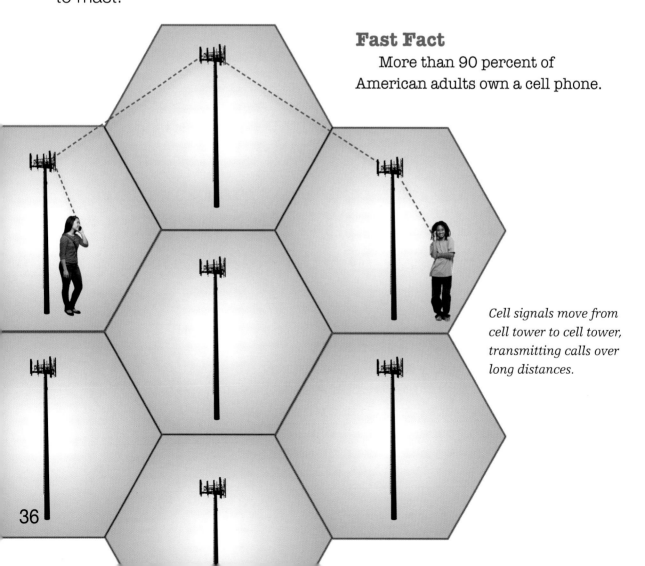

Fast Fact
More than 90 percent of American adults own a cell phone.

Cell signals move from cell tower to cell tower, transmitting calls over long distances.

Computers for business and home use led to the Internet as we know it. The Internet is made of tens of thousands of interconnected networks. These interconnected networks are run by service providers, companies, universities, and governments.

Early, room-sized computers were in use by 1939. They produced mathematical tables. The early models used vacuum tubes and punch cards for the computations. Later versions changed rapidly as technology developed.

The First Dot-Com

The first dot-com domain name was registered on March 15, 1985. After two years, only 100 dot-coms were registered. In 1990, Tim Berners-Lee developed HyperText Markup Language (HTML), leading to the World Wide Web.

Tim Berners-Lee's computer became the world's first web server.

During the following decades, companies continued to improve and develop new technologies to increase computer abilities.

In 1969, computer languages were developed and Intel produced the **microprocessor** for computers, while four universities introduced a link that became the Internet. Microprocessors are computer chips that run electrical devices.

The UNIVAC I (Universal Automatic Computer I) was the first commercial computer produced in the United States. It was used by the U.S. Census Bureau in 1951. The 46 computers eventually sold for over a million dollars each.

Bill Gates developed the microcomputer Basic in 1974. The computer mouse and personal computers followed. However, early prices were too costly for most individuals.

The bit is the smallest unit of information in the binary system. Eight bits make a byte, a complete unit that works or stores information. The electrical current interprets the bytes to make letters of numbers in digital code.

The electronic element in computers is the integrated circuit (IC) chip, a tiny microchip which holds multiple transistors. Computer transistors control electrical circuits. The circuits stand for information as numbers and letters. The current signals if the computer is on or off using the digital binary system, using 0s and 1s.

The years spanning 1975 to 1999 brought digital technology that radically changed the way people communicate. In 1981, the first personal computers became available. Digital storage increased with the development of DVDs (Digital Versatile Discs) and CDs (Compact Discs).

In 1990, HyperText Transfer Protocol (HTTP) was developed. It is the foundation of data communication for the World Wide Web. HyperText defines how messages are configured and transmitted, and what actions web servers and browsers should take in response to various commands.

Fast Fact

HDTV (High-Definition Television) was developed by 1998. Broadband Internet service was made available in 1999.

Tandy Radio Shack produced the first desktop computer, the TRS-80, in 1977. The 1980s brought improvements and more portability to computers, along with lower prices.

Since 2000, the Internet has revolutionized information exchange and entertainment. Digital e-books were introduced and the next year iPods came out. By 2002 all televisions could receive digital programming.

Steven Jobs brought out the first iPad tablet in 2010, a revolutionary idea

Seeds of Change

In 1977, Steve Wozniak and Steve Jobs started their new company, Apple Computer, Inc. They followed up the next year with the Apple II. Apple's innovations in communication technology have changed the world.

Steve Wozniac

Steve Jobs
1955 – 2011

Global Positioning System (GPS) is a navigation system based on 24 satellites put into orbit by the U.S. Department of Defense. It locates positions of objects and provides directions via interactive maps on smartphones and computers.

A U.S. Air Force service member oversees Global Positioning System satellite operations.

The GPS satellites orbit Earth twice a day. The transmitters send information to Earth. GPS receivers take in the information. They **triangulate** the location using three satellites, which means the GPS receiver compares the time of signal transmission with reception of at least three satellites. The time difference tells the receiver how far away the satellite is. The other satellites also provide distance measurements to pinpoint locations.

43

Imagine taking your smartphone back in time, to an era when written communications were hand-delivered and no one had heard of television. What might they think of the device in your hand when you show them everything it's capable of? From music, to movies, to instant messages, wave technology has transformed the ways the world communicates—and put the wonders of the world at your fingertips.

Timeline

1831: Joseph Henry invents the first electric telegraph.

1835: Samuel Morse develops the Morse code.

1873: James Clerk Maxwell discovers the electromagnetic field.

1876: Alexander Graham Bell patents the electric telephone.

1876: Emile Berliner invents the first microphone.

1877: Thomas Edison invents the cylinder-based phonograph.

1887: Emile Berliner invents the disk phonograph record.

1895: Guglielmo Marconi discovers radio signals.

1901: Marconi communicates across the Atlantic using radio signals.

1912: First radio broadcast; the Radio Act law passes.

1914: Hiram Percy Maxim founds the American Radio Relay League of amateur (ham) radio operators.

1916: Radios with different stations become available.

1921: Amateur radio reaches around the world.

1926: NBC establishes first radio broadcasting network.

1927: Philo Farnsworth sends the first television picture.

1941: Radio FM broadcasting from New York takes place, although it wasn't widespread until the 1950s.

1948: First regular broadcast of television shows by four networks, NBC, CBS, ABC, and DuMont.

1954: First color television sets developed and first transistor radio goes on sale.

1969: Computer languages are developed.

1973: The first cell phone system is developed.

1983: Cell phones are made available to public.

1993: World Wide Web goes public.

2001: Early communication devices like Palm OS, Blackberry OS, and Windows CE come on market.

2002: All televisions can receive digital programing and satellite radio launched.

2003: iTunes is made available.

2008: First availability of WiFi during airplane flights.

2010: iPad tablet hits the market; Skype is introduced; iPhone 4 and Facetime develop.

2012: Smartphone use reaches a billion people worldwide.

Glossary

amplitude (AM-pli-tood): the height of a wave

compression (kuhm-PRES-zhuhn): the location on a wave where the molecules are pushed very close together

electromagnetic waves (i-lek-troh-MAG-neh-tik WAYVZ): a form of radiant energy with differing wavelengths

frequency (FREE-kwuhn-see): how fast a wave is vibrating per second

integrated circuit (IN-ti-grate-uhd SUR-kit): a tiny microchip that holds large numbers of transistors

longitudinal (lahn-ji-TOO-duh-nuhl): waves moving parallel to the direction of the wave's motion

microprocessor (MYE-kroh-prah-ses-ur): microprocessors are computer chips used to run electrical devices

modulation (MAH-joo-lay-shuhn): varying the properties of a wave

oscillate (AWS-uh-late): a regular back and forth motion

pixels (PIKS-uhlz): all the available points on a grid

rarefaction (rair-uh-FAHK-shuhn): the location on a wave cycle where the molecules are spread far apart

spectrum (SPEK-truhm): a range between two particular points

transistors (tran-ZIS-tuhrs): small electronic switches and amplifiers

transverse (trans-vurhs): extending or situated across something

triangulate (trye-ANG-yoo-late): the process of comparing three different points to determine a location

Index

Show What You Know

1. Explain how mechanical waves differ from electromagnetic waves.
2. Discuss the significance of Marconi's discovery of radio waves.
3. Why is there a need for fast communication and how did it lead to the technology used today?
4. What is the relationship of wave size to the intensity?
5. In what way did computers change the way people communicate?

Websites to Visit

www.physicsclassroom.com/Physics-Interactives/Waves-and-Sound

www.acs.psu.edu/drussell/Demos/waves/wavemotion.html

www.visionlearning

About the Author

Shirley Duke enjoys communicating information by writing for young people, even though it isn't using waves. She does use information waves every day, especially for learning about new subjects and keeping up with friends. She lives in the Jemez Mountains of New Mexico with her husband.

Meet The Author!
www.meetREMauthors.com

© 2016 Rourke Educational Media

www.rourkeeducationalmedia.com

PHOTO CREDITS: Cover © bluebay, nmedia; Page 4 © DNY59, Wikipedia; Page 5 © Wikipedia, Charles Mann Photography, Page 6, 25 © jrabelo, Page 7, 8, 29 © Library of Congress; Page 9 © ktsdesign/Science Source; Page 10 © brunoil, Cathleen A Clapper; Page 12 © SCIENCE PHOTO LIBRARY; Page 16 © lchumpitaz, NASA; Page 17 © Moreno Soppelsa; Page 18 © TommylX; Page 19 © iDesign; Page 20 © alexsalcedo; Page 21 © NASA/JPL-Caltech, Wikipedia, United States Environmental Protection Agency; Page 22 © LIFE Photo Archive; Page 23 © MartinLisner; Page 24 © Everett Historical; Page 26 © i3alda; Page 27 © franckreporter; Page 28 © 3Dsculptor, Wikipedia, Bettmann/Corbis/AP Images; Page 29 © Bettmann/Corbis/AP Images; Page 30 © alexsl, AniLiang186682777408; Page 31 © SilverV; Page 32 © HultonArchive; Page 33 © Ew Chee Guan; Page 34 © ZargonDesign, sputnikos, ISerg; Page 35 © Matjaz Boncina; Page 36 © Aldo Murillo, Kalman Otto; Page 37 © Wikipedia; Page 38 © U.S. Census Bureau; Page 39 © St3fano; Page 40 Inaki Antonana; Page 41 © Lisa F. Young; Page 42 © Al Luckow, Wikipedia; Page 43 © Paul Fleet; Page 44 © Ashish Raj Shrestha

Edited by: Keli Sipperley

Cover design by: Nicola Stratford   www.nicolastratford.com

Interior design by: Jen Thomas

Library of Congress PCN Data

Information Waves / Shirley Duke
(Let's Explore Science)
ISBN 978-1-68191-391-9 (hard cover)
ISBN 978-1-68191-433-6 (soft cover)
ISBN 978-1-68191-472-5 (e-Book)
Library of Congress Control Number: 2015951558

Also Available as: